Cursive Handwriting

Practice Workbook

Children's Reading & Writing Education Books

Left Brain Kids

Educational Books for Children

Practice Cursive Writing

Trace and rewrite the words below.

able   able

able   able

above   above

above   above

Trace and rewrite the words below.

afraid *able*

able *able*

afternoon *afternoon*

afternoon *afternoon*

Trace and rewrite the words below.

again   *again*

again   *again*

age   *age*

age   *age*

Trace and rewrite the words below.

air   *air*

air   *air*

airplane   *airplane*

airplane   *airplane*

Trace and rewrite the words below.

almost   almost

almost   almost

alone   alone

alone   alone

Trace and rewrite the words below.

along   *along*

along   *along*

already   *already*

already   *already*

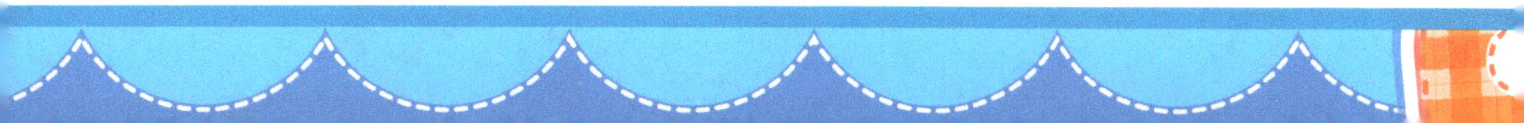

Trace and rewrite the words below.

also   also

also   also

always   always

always   always

Trace and rewrite the words below.

animal   *animal*

animal   *animal*

another   *another*

another   *another*

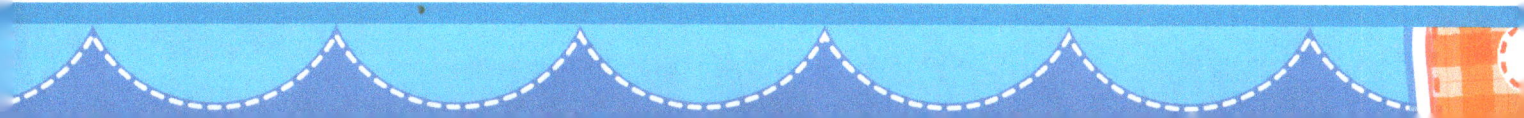

Trace and rewrite the words below.

anything   anything

anything   anything

around   around

around   around

art   art

art   art

aunt   aunt

aunt   aunt

Trace and rewrite the words below.

balloon   balloon

balloon   balloon

bark   bark

bark   bark

Trace and rewrite the words below.

barn   barn

barn   barn

basket   basket

basket   basket

Trace and rewrite the words below.

beach   beach

beach   beach

bear   bear

bear   bear

Trace and rewrite the words below.

because   *because*

because   *because*

become   *become*

become   *become*

Trace and rewrite the words below.

began   began

began   began

begin   begin

begin   begin

Trace and rewrite the words below.

behind   behind

behind   behind

believe   believe

believe   believe

Trace and rewrite the words below.

below   below

below   below

belt   believe

believe   believe

better   *better*

better   *better*

birthday   *believe*

believe   *believe*

Trace and rewrite the words below.

body   body

body   body

bones   bones

bones   bones

Trace and rewrite the words below.

born   born

born   born

bought   bought

bought   bought

Trace and rewrite the words below.

bread   bread

bread   bread

bright   bright

bright   bright

broke

broke

broke

broke

brought

brought

brought

brought

Trace and rewrite the words below.

busy   busy

busy   busy

cabin   cabin

cabin   cabin

Trace and rewrite the words below.

cage   cage

cage   cage

camp   camp

camp   camp

Trace and rewrite the words below.

can't   can't

can't   can't

care   care

care   care

Trace and rewrite the words below.

carry   carry

carry   carry

catch   catch

catch   catch

Trace and rewrite the words below.

cattle   cattle

cattle   cattle

cave   cave

cave   cave

Trace and rewrite the words below.

children   *children*

children   *children*

class   *class*

class   *class*

close   close

close   close

cloth   cloth

cloth   cloth

Trace and rewrite the words below.

coal   coal

coal   coal

color   color

color   color

Trace and rewrite the words below.

corner   corner

corner   corner

cotton   cotton

cotton   cotton

Trace and rewrite the words below.

cover   cover

cover   cover

dark   dark

dark   dark

Trace and rewrite the words below.

desert   desert

desert   desert

didn't   didn't

didn't   didn't

Trace and rewrite the words below.

dinner   dinner

dinner   dinner

dishes   dishes

dishes   dishes

Trace and rewrite the words below.

does   does

does   does

done   done

done   done

Good Job!

www.ingramcontent.com/pod-product-compliance
Lightning Source LLC
Chambersburg PA
CBHW081233020426
42331CB00012B/3155